DR. ROBERT KANDARJIAN

SACRED INTENTIONS

2008

Sacred Intentions

TABLE OF CONTENTS

INTRODUCTION

During my twenty-four year practice, I have had the privilege of listening to some of the most inspiring as well as tragic stories. I consider my patients extremely brave and soulful; and therefore, I consider myself blessed. Some have revealed narratives that would weave a Tolstoy novel and move large men to tears. I view their perseverance as an inspiring testament to the spiritual optimism that resides within us all. Their revelations charged with desires and intentions, and resulting in both triumphs and disappointments, have shaped their values, beliefs and drives. I am doubly blessed because I have been an ear and a witness to their courageous human dramas. They have been my teachers as I still remain a student.

Over the years, I found myself conversing with patients about a common topic and theme with great zest and satisfaction, undoubtedly to my benefit as well as theirs. The topic was about intentions or what I call "conscious desire". How does one learn to define one's intentions, how does one know which intentions will bare fruits, how does one go about manifesting those intentions, and how does God help?

In this book, I have attempted to condense those discussions into fourteen intentions. I believe these fourteen intentions express the deepest longings of our unfolding spiritual journey. Through this book, I hope many of you resonate with the outlined intentions and discover the hidden greatness and courage within your soul.

A PRIVATE HOLY PLACE

In God We Trust" is stamped on all U.S. bills and coins. Do we really trust God? This is perhaps the most private and challenging journey that we are all embarking upon here on Earth.

A good place to start this journey is to find that one thing that helps you connect to what you feel God is: a sacred place, nature, a song, a color, etc...Visit daily this "private holy place" and remain in the quiet and silent room within yourself that emanates with peace and self-acceptance. These "holy" visitations gradually reduce the chatter of the mind and increase our faith in the Divine Force.

There is within us all an intuitive knowing, a gut knowledge or instinct which protects us and guides us to fulfilling decisions. In our "private holy place" we can hear, see, feel, smell, taste and sense this knowing which is God's voice, a voice that can be trusted. Happiness happens when we make good decisions. The more we visit our "private holy place", the better decisions we make and the greater our trust in God.

Therefore, let us place our faith in the voice of our gut knowing and not dismiss its power and validity. Our gut knowing is a reality and an experience that transcends the emotions and the logical mind. It is similar to a calm lake that possesses a certainty, clarity, and a peace unknown to the overactive mind and swaying emotions. It is in this still lake where we find God and learn that trust in God comes from trusting our inner knowing.

In the sanctuary of our "private holy place" we fully receive inner calm and the guidance to balance our lives. We learn to balance giving with receiving, empathy with detachment, work with play, thinking with feeling, surrender with control, tenderness with assertion, vulnerability with courage, the child with the adult, and the feminine with the masculine. As we balance these elements of our lives by trusting the guiding voice of our inner sacred knowing, we create better decisions and therefore happiness. By trusting God, life's movement sends our way all the tools that are needed to gently and harmoniously create meaning and joy in daily life.

Trusting God is a personal journey that takes patience and practice. The practice is to allow ourselves to receive the guidance of our gut knowing from our "private holy place". The patience requires that we explore our relationship with God to discover our spiritual identity and purpose on Earth. Our relationship with God and inner knowing is one and the same; to trust one is to trust the other, and it is this trust which makes life an easier and a more satisfying journey.

Namaste`

INTENTION 1
I declare an intention to trust and to live my intuition.

Whenever my intuition speaks and reveals itself, I declare an intention to trust and honor its voice. I do not jump to my head and question the validity of my intuition. My intuition is the wise-self within me that guides me to my happiness. I always listen to the wise-self within me.

My intuition is always valid when I am in a state of peace and calm. My intuition, which rises from my stillness, is the voice of my Higher-Self guiding me to my true soul longings and happiness.

I best hear, sense, and feel my intuition when I am still. I can be still in a sanctuary, a park, by a lake, a backyard, in my room, or from music. It is important for me to explore what surroundings and environment best helps promote and nurture my stillness. I practice stillness by remaining quiet and silencing the chatter of my thoughts and overthinking. My stillness calms my nerves and sooths my worries; it heals my cells and quiets my mind. From my stillness I can hear my intuition and therefore create more with less effort. My stillness connects me to my intuition and teaches me how to live from a place of effortlessness and ease.

It is from my intuition that the reservoir of guidance, wisdom and harmony unfold. I declare an intention to honor and live from my intuition. It is not enough that I hear and trust my intuition; I must also learn to act and live my life from it. I surround myself with supportive people who help me live from my intuition.

My intuition gives me the tools to manifest my soul's longings. My intuition helps me make great decisions. I always trust my intuition and live from it.

INTENTION 2
I declare an intention to unconditionally surrender to Divine Will.

The more I surrender to Divine Will the more control I have over my life. Allowing Divine Will to unite and align with mine is a gift I welcome and celebrate. Divine Will is identical to my soul's will; what my soul wants for me is what Divine Will wants for me. Divine Will knows intimately and accurately what decisions and direction are best for my soul.

Divine Will knows better than my human will which path and course of action my life should take. My human will and personality live in confusion at times, and aren't always clear what desires and needs are best for me. The desires of my personality are endless and not always satisfying; I want to connect with my soul desires to express who I really am. My purpose and destiny on Earth is to live my soul's desires and longings, therefore; I unconditionally surrender to Divine Will. By surrendering to Divine Will my life finds clarity, direction and purpose.

I silence the chatter of my mind and surrender to my body's guidance and wisdom. I unconditionally surrender to Divine Will through silence. I hear Divine Will by remaining silent and listening to the intuitive messages, which emanate from my body. In silence, I ask for guidance and surrender. The sole purpose of Divine Will is to assure my happiness. I continually remain connected to my Divine Will. Divine Will is the pilot guiding me to my joy and to the longings I want to experience and express.

INTENTION 3
I declare an intention to ask for help and know that it is safe and fun.

There is no reason for me to go through my personal growth process alone. There are many wonderful, competent and caring people besides family and dear friends who can lend a helping hand when I am in distress. Doing it alone is lengthy, painful, and unnecessary. I don't have to do it alone. My intention is to become more comfortable asking for help. I want to experience a life in which I have a safety net of people who nurture and comfort me during challenging times.

To be fully present on Earth, the feeling of safety and fun must run through every cell of my body. I create safety by the company I keep, the joy I draw from my work and hobbies, and the trust and faith I have in God and myself.

My gut knowing or inner voice guides me to the right people. My gut knowing tells me who feels safe to reveal myself to. I trust my gut knowing. Safety is the most crucial ingredient I look for when scanning for help. Healing can only and should only take place in an environment of safety. My gut knowing and my reasoning mind acting as two scanners guide me and watch over me. I am safe in my asking because I honor the reliability of my gut knowing and the strength of my reasoning mind.

As I become more comfortable in asking for human and Divine help, my earthly and heavenly support systems continue to build and solidify. The more support I allow myself to receive, the more safety and joy I feel in daily life. The more safety I feel in my life, the more fun I experience. The support, safety, and fun help me connect deeper with my purpose, direction, strength, and passion. It is comforting to know there is always a safety net of people who nurture me, and a benevolent Universe that watches over me.

INTENTION 4
I declare an intention to balance giving with receiving.

As I develop my trust in my intuitive abilities through meditation and prayer, it becomes easier to determine from whom I want to receive and to whom I want to give. To receive from another implies that I trust and surrender to the kindness, wisdom and skills of the other; and to give, I follow and remain true to my inner guidance.

Through silence and meditation, I become clear of the things I must let go of in order to open the receiving channels in my heart and mind. As I receive clarity, awareness, and faith, I release the fears that block the receiving of abundance, comfort, and hope. I want to receive only those things that are for my highest good and that serve to further my development and evolution.

As I receive the abundance that is my birthright, I am filled with Light and therefore more able to give to others who are open to receiving. I give discriminately; I give to those who can appreciate my giving and have the capacity to receive. My intuition guides my giving so that my giving serves the soul needs of the other. When my intuition tells me to not give, I do not; I hold back and wait for further intuitive guidance. I honor my guidance though I may not always understand it. I do not give when my energy is low and when I feel depleted. I refuel myself through rest to fill my tank before I resume giving. I always remember to give to myself and to refuel.

My body will always remind me when I am out of balance between giving and receiving. I listen to my body. Giving love, support, guidance and material help to others brings me joy and delight. The reward is in seeing others benefit from my giving. As I give, I also remain open to receiving from others the good they have to offer. From receiving, I replenish myself; I learn surrendering and humility, and I continue to strengthen my bonds with others.

When strangers need my giving or choose to give to me, I honor and follow my intuitive voice in such exchanges. My intuitive voice tells me from whom I should receive and to whom I should give. Receiving is a passive mode that allows me to surrender to another's giving, and giving is an active mode that allows others to surrender to my giving.

I never forget to give to myself and refuel.

INTENTION 5
I declare an intention to nurture myself.

Nurturing myself means that I do things that are good for my physical, mental, emotional and spiritual growth. By taking the time to go inward on a daily basis, I realign myself with my energy flow and inner voice. My inner voice guides me to how I can best nurture myself.

I nurture myself in all areas of my life: career, family, friends, physical health, social, cultural and spiritual activities, and much more. It is important to determine which area of nurturance is most critical for a particular day, week or month. My inner voice instructs me as to which area needs most nurturance at a specific juncture of my life.

Nurturing myself also means that I ask for help from others as well as God, for I am open to receive. There is no reason for me to do it all alone when the kindness and skills of others are available. The quiet time I spend alone to align and connect with my energy flow and inner voice is the most important means by which I nurture myself. My inner gauge tells me whether I am on empty or on full and how I can best remain full.

A powerful way in which I nurture myself is by saying No to associations that are unhealthy and invitations which my instincts reject. By saying No to those things that are not for the best interest of my soul, I open the "Yes" door to prospects and opportunities that can and will materialize my soulful intentions, dreams and plans. As I remain committed to nurturing my body, mind and soul, my happiness multiplies and my relationships fill with Light.

My inner voice guides me to my self-nurturance.

INTENTION 6
I declare an intention to unconditionally forgive myself and release all self-blame.

A s a spiritual being on earth learning and growing, it is likely that I'll make mistakes, for I am human. I see and hold the mistakes as growing opportunities. The mystics say mistakes are the bumpy road to God. I unconditionally forgive myself for the past, because with the maturity that I possessed in the past, I made the best decisions I could. If I could have made better decisions, I would have. To not forgive myself means to freeze the energy of a past event in my body and cells and become drained, dejected, and frozen in the past. By forgiving myself, I liberate the frozen energy to restore vitality and joy in my body and life. God is not a punishing and unforgiving God. God wants me to forgive myself as long as I have learned from my remorse and gained wisdom from my past. As I unconditionally forgive myself, I move closer to my heart with humility and self-love, and feel the desire and zest for life and living.

My past mistakes do not define my total being. I am more than the "mistake". I balance my life by remembering my contributions, generosity, and benevolence. I also recall how I have brought joy to others. Forgiving myself is a process that may take time. I honor the time needed, knowing that I do not have to take the journey alone. I have God, my self-compassion, and the compassion of others leading me to greater degrees of self-forgiveness.

INTENTION 7
I declare an intention to unconditionally forgive others and release blame.

I unconditionally forgive others because not forgiving others compromises my immune system and makes me emotionally, spiritually, mentally, and physically ill. I recognize that I am a magnet and I attract experiences. If I have attracted a painful and negative experience, it means there are lessons I am still learning. I ask for God's help to minimize the painful experiences and to give me the strength to forgive others. Not forgiving others prevents me from seeing the lessons, the wisdom, and the growth offered by that experience.

Living with non-forgiveness draws more negative people and negative energies into my life. I choose and want to attract and draw only those experiences that nurture my soul. Blaming others keeps me locked in an imprisoned past and prevents me from learning from past events and negative patterns. Ultimately, non-forgiveness closes my heart and takes away the softness of my being. I choose to remain open with my heart, knowing that I can also be firm and assertive whenever needed. I choose to live a life of balance between softness and positive assertion.

Forgiveness does not mean that I must continue a relationship that does not serve me. I don't have to be fond of a person in order to forgive them. I want my soul and their soul to be in acquiescence. Forgiveness helps me make peace with myself and reconcile with another's soul. As I forgive others, I cleanse my soul and body cells from entrapment, stagnation and illness. Through forgiveness I move out from a trapped and frozen past and move into a promising future.

INTENTION 8
I declare an intention to dissolve all self-doubt.

Whenever self-doubt raises its head, I do my best to remain in my strength and power. My faith in God assures me that doubts are stumbling blocks and teachers that will soon disappear.

To maintain and support my faith in myself during times of self-doubt, I recognize, appreciate, and acknowledge my past triumphs, achievements, and accomplishments. I readily reach out for help to those who have the skill, wisdom and heart to help me return to assurance, faith in life, and faith in myself.

I recognize that doubts by nature are present in our lives to help strengthen our faith in God, in others and in us. Doubts are a way through which we link, bond and connect to Spirit, to humanity and to our inner strength. The good news is that doubts are temporary and in time they become clarified and dissolved. I see time as a cherished ally that unfolds the truth of certainty in its own perfect pace. I do not make hasty decisions when I am in self-doubt; I stay grounded and take my time in order to make fruitful and positive decisions. Time helps me gently and lovingly towards self-assurance. In time and with the counsel of wise and supportive people in my life, all my self-doubts disappear.

When I fully, totally, and completely trust God, my self-doubts and my fears minimize and eventually disappear. Trust in God changes my doubtful mental state to certainty and optimism, and my fearful emotional state to peace and courage. When I dissolve self-doubt, I make life-enhancing and effective decisions.

INTENTION 9
I declare an intention to grow through joy
rather than struggle and pain.

Whenever I am confronted with a stressful or challenging situation, I see it as an opportunity to grow. I know growth does not have to be with pain and struggle. When I pay attention to life's signs and signals, I can avoid a crisis or at least minimize its impact. I am learning from life's signs and signals by recognizing my patterns, honoring my intuition and gut feelings, asking for help, coming out of blaming, and remaining in gratitude and faith. I further grow by paying attention to sound reason, reading helpful books, avoiding negative people, saying no when needed, and yes when appropriate. All the above tools help me to grow through joy and avoid crisis, pain and struggle. The joy unfolds when I take baby steps in making the necessary changes. I am gentle with myself when I falter knowing I am human; thus, I forgive myself for my mistakes and errors. I don't quit.

Pain and struggle are coarse and loud teachers. I choose to learn from a gentler teacher, I choose to learn from joy. The time I allocate for introspection and meditation assures me an increased awareness of my patterns and errors. I carefully examine and explore my past hurts and struggles to better understand patterns that no longer serve me. I don't curse my past wounds, but rather I view them as teachers guiding me to a life of greater self-awareness and effortless joy.

INTENTION 10
I declare an intention to see and feel the
cooperative spirit of humanity.

C ontrary to planetary beliefs about scarcity, there is an abundance of land, food, shelter, love and safety. This plenitude and abundance increases when the spirit of humanity engages in greater cooperation and collaboration. Remembering we are all from the same source, we will hoard, compete, and steal no more.

Cooperation takes place when we acknowledge our primal and basic similarities that we are all children of God and an expression of the Divine Plan. We are here to experience our sacred potentials and to serve one another. Once we recognize that the greatest joy is in helping others experience their innate and inherent power, we will create greater safety and joy for ourselves. To see and feel the cooperative spirit of humanity, I daily go inward and learn how to best cooperate with my inner voice, for this is where sacred cooperation begins.

Malice and evil emerge when an individual is not in cooperation with his or her inner voice. The greatest gift that we can offer others is to guide and teach them to cooperate with their inner voice. As we all know, it is totally natural for children to live from their inner voice; therefore, we must encourage, support, and assure that healthy behavior. As we live our lives from our inner voice, it becomes easier for us to help others do the same. To spread the cooperative spirit of humanity, we must be spiritual examples and cooperate with our own inner voice, which is the voice of God inside of us.

INTENTION 11
I declare an intention to not own another's pain.

I maintain my boundaries by recognizing that the pain of others must remain within their own boundaries and skin. I sit with love and compassion for those who suffer, but I do not absorb their pain and become the sufferer. By remaining within my boundaries, I am able to remain objective and grounded when I am around the pain of others. My objectivity and grounding keep me in my center and within my own skin, and therefore, help give me the focus to effectively serve others.

My faith tells me that God shares their pain and that they are always in God's hands. Therefore, I no longer place their pain in my body and soul; I place their pain in a Divine Container and offer it to God for healing and transformation.

By not absorbing the pain of others, I create the space for them to own their pain. By owning their pain, they create the opportunity to learn and grow from the pain. They learn the qualities of courage, self-acceptance, and self-confidence; and they grow into greater awareness and independence.

Their pain is perhaps bringing forth important and deep lessons about their ineffective patterns and negative beliefs. When I own their pain, I take away their lessons and delay their growth process. I am aware that owning their pain leaves me depleted and resentful; therefore, I declare an intention to allow others to own their pain.

By staying in my heart and in my assertion, I gently challenge the adults in my life to own their pain. My intention is to maintain and hold my boundaries and help guide others toward healthy personal boundaries with the world and with me.

INTENTION 12
I declare an intention to strengthen my spiritual faith.

Spiritual faith is all around us. As co-creators, we created all that we see, feel, taste, smell, touch and hear. The miracle of creation restores my faith in God with the concrete knowledge that we are never alone. The Divine realm watches over us as long as we are open to receive that which is for our highest good. The journey of spiritual faith is remembering we are Divine beings in physical forms.

My faith operates on four levels: faith in God, faith in others, faith in myself, and faith in tomorrow or the future.

I strengthen my faith in God through silence, stillness, meditation, prayer, tithing, and gratitude. As a seeker, my search for God takes precedence and therefore, I make time to be with God on daily basis. My faith in others increases as I trust my intuition and gut feelings. My positive gut feelings lead me to people, situations and experiences that I can trust and that are safe. The more I honor my intuitive voice the more I am led to situations and relationships that can be trusted. My faith in others is a result of my faith in my intuitive voice and gut feelings. By trusting my inner voice, I attract relationships that can be trusted and that are safe.

My faith in myself begins with acknowledging, recognizing and appreciating my talents, accomplishments, achievements and triumphs. Having friends, counselors, and family members who value my contributions and presence increases my faith in myself; therefore, I only invite into my life those relationships that nurture my self-value and self-worth. I do not indulge in negative self-judgment and self-criticism for my errors and mistakes for they are ultimately lessons in wisdom. I forgive myself for my past, knowing that I have done the best that I could and I am now doing the best that I can.

My faith in tomorrow and the future grows and multiplies as I continue to feel supported and comforted by God, by others, and by my faith in my strength and humility.

INTENTION 13
I declare an intention to learn from pain and suffering.

When a crisis strikes, I ask Spirit to help me learn the necessary lessons from the pain and suffering caused by the crisis. It is a spiritual law that no suffering is in vain. I acknowledge that crises are shaking and releasing outdated and limiting belief systems and thought patterns about life, love, relationships, illness, family, money, and much more. I reduce my pain and suffering by regular introspection and meditation. I am not afraid to ask for assistance and support from God, counselors, and from loved ones during painful periods in my life. I try to gain wisdom from the crises to expand my self-awareness and self-understanding.

By learning from pain and suffering, I slowly move out of blaming myself, blaming others and blaming God. I know that any kind of blaming and non-forgiveness keep me stuck in the past and prevent me from moving into the future. From pain and suffering I learn and develop empathy, patience, strength, faith, appreciation, intelligence, intuition and many other noble and spiritual qualities and traits. These qualities and traits in turn will help me prevent future hardships, pain and suffering.

In spite of all the pain and suffering, I choose to hold on to and maintain my balance between my tenderness and my power. The suffering has not closed off my heart to joy and love nor has it depleted or relinquished my assertion and power. I remain loving as well as brave, embracing life's gifts and pleasures.

INTENTION 14
I declare an intention to be my Higher Self.

My higher self is the divine part of me as well as the largest part of me. My higher self knows no fear because it is one with God. When fears and anxieties surface, my higher self helps me recognize that those fears and anxieties are there to help me grow into my individuality, humanity and divinity. My higher self helps me feel my fears in a contained and loving space to flourish my growth and my strength.

My higher self reminds me that we are all inter-connected as souls whose source is One. My higher self keeps me connected to the higher purpose of service here on earth. It reminds me to honor and respect each person's soul journey. My relationship with others is with their higher selves and therefore satisfying and enriching. Whatever best serves the higher self of others best serves me; therefore, I live in a spirit of cooperation and rapture. My higher self watches over me, protects me, guides me and consoles me.

4703575R0

Sacred Intentions

Dear Diandra   Aug-17-2011

A joy to know you

and I'm grateful.

R.